Achilles the

ISBN: 978-1-914458-27-9
Published by P2D Books Ltd

Designed and typeset by Ray Wilkinson
Printed in Great Britain by P2D Books Limited

Cover images
Front: Head of Aphaia, National Museum on Aegina, Greece
Back: Mycenaean necklace, National Museum on Kos, Greece

Achilles the Changeling
Judith Foster

.

Contents

Before the story begins:

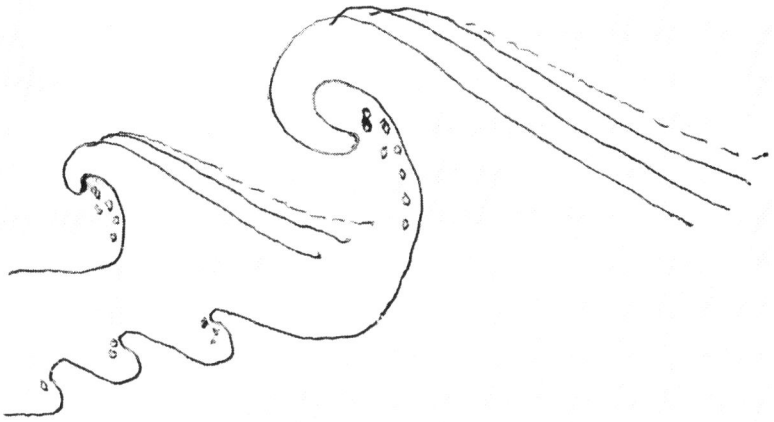

Halfway through the Trojan War, Achilles, the warrior hero, and King Agamemnon, general of all the Greek forces, made a pact, whereby Agamemnon would command the land forces, and Achilles the thousand-strong fleet. They swore to seal the pact with the marriage of Agamemnon's daughter Iphigeneia to Achilles. But at Aulis on the shore of the Gulf of Evvia, as they prepared to sail back to Troy, they failed to honour properly the goddess Artemis. She, in a rage, drove a tempestuous wind against them to prevent their sailing. To placate her, Agamemnon sacrificed Iphigeneia at Artemis's altar on the shore.

The Gleeful Gods

And so, these mortals mess among our plans

Come, raise a cup, let's watch what hatches down below
At Aulis. The great king's second sally
To strong-walled Troy, to strike the final blow;
The army's there, the fleet, caïque and galley
Prepared to sail, but helpless now against
Storms raised from nowhere. Artemis, goddess,
By the neglect of proper rites incensed,
Invokes wild, southern winds, impeding their progress.
And so these mortals mess among our plans,
Tipping the scales now to Mycenae, now

To Ithaca, now to the king of Spartans,
Thinking that they direct high fortune's flow,
And through their little acts control the great.
Artemis in a huff made strong winds drive
The thudding tempest from the south. That strait
Is difficult at best. No man alive
Could navigate the rocks and hidden reeves
Through those tumultuous waves, nor could predict
Whence the next wave, the buffet comes that thieves
His judgement, so his ship fouls derelict.

Artemis, wilful, resented insult's stings.
Did she demand the daughter's sacrifice?
Or was it a conspiracy of kings
To rid themselves of one who was too nice
On points of honour, duties and dues?
Iphigeneia, promised to Achilles,
Seemed to that man the prize that he would choose
Among the treasures of his pledged allies.
He would put off his moodiness, not sulk,
Co-operate as admiral joint in power
With Agamemnon; with the mighty bulk
Of his one thousand fleet cause Troy to cower.

Look, they deck the milk-white bull with flowers,
Red garlands, wreaths of oak between his horns
Sheathed with gold. He, bridled, pawing, glowers
At the near-naked girl, crowned with hot thorns,
Who hides her body on his hairy flank,
Yet holds her head high; at her hideous fate
She does not quail; sees among the men of rank
Achilles horrified, comfort too late
To save or to console her sacrifice.
He steps back quietly, turns about his heel.

The fire of hot Achilles chills to ice.
His loyalty to Greece he will repeal.

Two ways to live we gods had offered him:
The glory of the hero's gilded life
Cut off at midday, famed in song and hymn;
Or anonymity devoid of strife.
This was his choice, each part attractive
This side or other of his dual mind.
He's had some glory. Now become passive
To his estates he'll go. Perhaps some peace he'll find.
And as for Troy, he never was the key
To its defeat. We plotted that his span
Should end before Troy's fall. Other eyes will see
The crumbling walls. Another worthy man
Will pull the rivets from the Trojan lock.
We've set a different scheme on course,
Trickier, less heroic, makes a mock
Of those who think strength is the only force.

Conspiracy

We'll give her a bull and your daughter

Oh, Agamemnon's a bully-boy,
And Odysseus cheats at dice.
To Agamemnon a body's a toy;
Odysseus will turn coat in a trice;
So what's with Menelaus?
He would just like to be nice.

'We've had enough of tantrums
From the unpredictable man
Who slides from peak to doldrums,
The crazed Thessalian

Whose brilliance sets the tactics,
But won't complete the plan.

He must be first of first;
Of equals, not enough.
Look, how the wind's gone south,
The sea'll be high and rough.
Let's offer Achilles a woman,
A bride, a crafty bluff.

Agamemnon, your daughter,
Are you willing to risk her tears?
Iphigeneia, worth cities,
But really, she's past her best years.
If Achilles, the mad, bad hero
Accepts her, my plan I'll make clear.

Artemis is angry, we forgot her.
So the seas in their violent career
Lash the wave-foam high over the mast-tops,
And the passage is too hard to steer.
So, we should offer the goddess
A gift to make the winds veer.

We'll give her a bull and your daughter,
Deny him his bride by her slaughter.
He'll withdraw, and we'll get our calm water.'

Achilles on the Shore

They spat contempt on what I had achieved

S he was promised to me.
She was promised mine:
Agamemnon's daughter,
Pivot of our design.
He, general of our armies,
I, admiral of the line,
In dominance of land and sea
Through her in blood combine
To make a new alliance,
A new empire define.

But Odysseus, the cur that hind me creeps,
Snake that winds itself into my reason,
Spider whose tangling legs enmesh my steps,
He knows my heart enough to hallow treason.
Plausible, vain and envious of my prowess,
Plotted with general and the brother
To use my bride as bait to charm the goddess
Who'd turned the sweet north wind to dirty weather.

I watched the girl tied to the snowy bull
Walk blind the beach down to Artemis' altar:
Iphigeneia, cast off, sacrificial;
Noble, lovely, Agamemnon's daughter.

They killed my bride.
I fled to hide
My shattered pride,
And to decide
Where I should bide.

I will not stay with them. They spat contempt
On what I had achieved before we came
To Aulis. Take the other choice, pre-empt
Their further treachery. I am not tame:
I am Achilles still. My Myrmidons,
My fifty ships, less one for me to sail,
Patroclus can now command those squadrons.
I will away to Thessaly. I will prevail.

Desolation

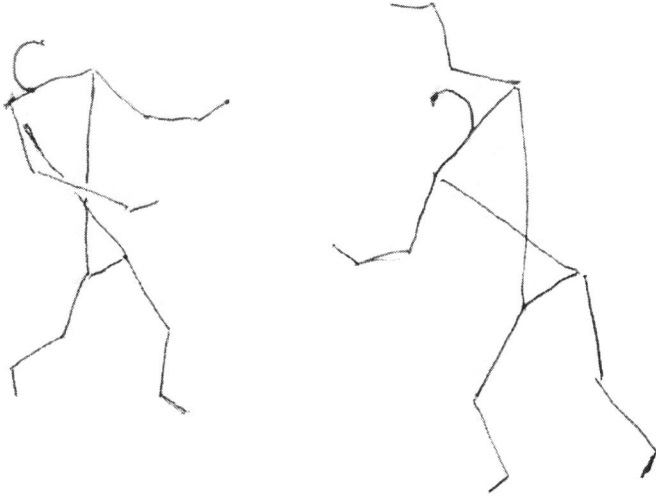

Creeps at dawn among his tents

He did not wait to see what happened on the beach.
His nauseous gut out-hollowed by the breach
Of trust, of what he'd thought was loyalty
Among the kings of Argos, perjured royalty,
Now swamped both fire and ice, fouled mind and body
To doddering puppet, flaccid, shoddy,
Swallowed his resolution, made him weak;
Not god-graced hero of the past, but unmanned freak.

He sweated and slept, now needs to find a haven.
So, creeps at dawn among his tents, craven,

To find his friend, his comfort, Patroclus,
To cradle and console, to soothe, meticulous
In care and love, the fractured soul, perhaps impart
IIow great Achilles may redeem his heart.

Patroclus watches as Achilles comes
Up through the rough flowered grass where loud the
                                        bronze bee hums,
And grey cicadas, leaping, knock against his knees
Stitched with white sword-scars, marks that itch and tease,
Puckering his skin, bee-tanned and ravaged
By years of war. But yet the ankle's still undamaged.

The boyhood friend, lover, companion to the man
Chokes down his tears, stretches his arms full open.
Patroclus, no less shocked than he before
The appalling sacrifice exacted on the shore,
Gathers him, warms him, feeds him with food and kindness,
Watches him sleep again in his distress,
Twitching in fever; and worries what to do
To help this mighty, toppled warrior, see him safely through
Beyond the reach of hurt from the destructive act.
Patroclus knows he's fragile, may react
In violence or apathy, untempered
By thought or reason, humanity dismembered.
For him, Patroclus schemes up a prophetic dream:
Hermes' alternative will make it seem
The right and proper route for him to take
Out of his gulf of nothingness, and calmly wake
To the new life laid out before him by the gods
Who had weighed out in equal parts the odds:
A life of tolerance, prosperity,
Renown all unremembered for eternity.

Patroclus concocts his dream, now must play the priest.
He wakes his friend, who slept till daylight ceased,
With urgent news he has interpreted
From Hermes' false, dreamed visit, who skimmed, buffeted
On those same waves roused to confound the perjured kings,
Where he, lifted by fluttering, sea-foam wings
Offers Achilles the promise of a life
Honeyed with favour, and unbloodied by war-strife.

Achilles wakes, rigid, trapped in angry muscles;
Beating in his head, blood's dark corpuscles
Throb and thrill and drum his ears and brain,
While blackened honour shrills his torment once again.
His friend's warm heart, light hand cools his sweaty shoulder.
The palpitating beat quietens; order,
A less impassioned view of what's been wrought
Returns and stills the turmoil of his churning thought.

Patroclus brings him honey, curded milk and rusk.
Achilles listens, owl-eyed in the dusk,
To what his wise friend relays of his dream,
And an interpretation that may spread a beam
Of light on his beleaguered soul, his troubled sprite.
He knows that from some source his mind took blight;
He wonders why he has no self-control;
He wonders why he's split inside, damaged, unwhole.
He longs to be released, unstrapped from destiny,
A middle way between black mutiny
And his blazing, incandescent brilliance
As he twists taut the anger to invite the chance
Of slashing, killing, mutilating that man's limb
Who never till that moment threatened him.
Is this shock from the kings in truth a jolt
Delivered by the god-of-gods' life-changing bolt?

Patroclus tells him how Hermes urged him to persuade
Tortured Achilles to outflank the shade
Of his twinned, warring minds and hear the call,
Not Troy's, but his own country's; there make his land-fall.

As Patroclus talks on, inside Achilles' head
Appears a well-known coast, a well-loved spread
Of sun-daubed landscape, rich with trees between,
Where youthful, he saw Peleus king and Thetis queen
Harvesting riches and reason, carefully just;
Restraining cheats, promoting such as must
Bring honour to the realm. He sees himself
Their heir, for his land's benefit accruing wealth.

Weighing the Choice

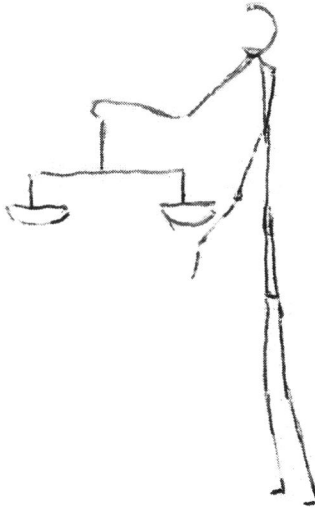

What profit's that to me?

What shall I lose now I have much to gain?
To lose a blood-stained, tumbled wreath
Perched on my head, the threnody's refrain
When comrades bear my limp corpse from the heath?
A hero's song through all eternity
Sung and recited bardly in the world?
What profit's that to me? Just vanity,
Praise for a violent life, a curse unfurled.
And gain? That same life nightly stitched with sleep,
Not wakeful, dreading an opponent's stealth;

Sweet, fragrant days, watching my country reap
The benefit as allies bring her wealth.
Thessaly's rich, seeded with flocks; skilled men
Make treasures, conjure jewels from her caves,
Her women make fine sons, and will again;
Defenders of our honour, each one braves
Those who would undermine our cities' peace.
We will obey the gods, make sacrifice
Without the blood of girls, respect, increase
The holy shrines, the oracle's advice.

When I was young, the gods gave me a choice
Between a hero's life with death at Troy,
Where glory, adulation would entice,
And calm, embedded peace that I'd enjoy
To a great age, rule at home with wisdom,
Reputation, stately guests, great and least,
Friends who'd promote the fortune of my kingdom
With fire, and food, and song in heart-warm feast.

Now is the moment when I can decide,
Knowing more my weakness, and what's my strength
Than ever I knew in my green spring-tide.
Injustice rots my heart. I'll trudge the length
Of all the plains of Greece to reach my land,
Shake off my wholesome anger gainst the kings
And practise...
But as I turn to wave a hand
I see what I shall lose: those precious things
That are my friend, that are my Patroclus:
His kindness to me over all these years;
His hands, when I am mad, he lays them thus,
Both sides my hammering head; he dulls the sneers
Of mocking Agamemnon, mockery

That still torments me, jeering at my youth
Spent among girls, whose fawning flattery
Hid my humiliation, hid the truth.

Can I leave Patroclus, my anchoring rock?
How will I do when high excitement flares
And my resistance crumbles with the shock
Of overwhelming anger, that ensnares
My body and my mind, slashing the first man comes,
Or woman, or a dog, the object's nil,
The action's all; tumultuous power drums
Me on in violence, till all in me's still?
Who then will save me from that brutal rage?
Will the gods help?

Will the gods help? Shall I seek Delphi's aid?
Sail north while Artemis will yet engage
Diminishing southern winds before they fade?

I must decide. There's no place here for me,
The kings, my enemies. Another's ships
Will lead the fleet to Troy; the wine-dark sea
No longer my domain; no more blood drips
From the honed point of my sword,
No more Achilles flawed
By the flawed union
Of parents in contention.

Departure

Patroclus, Achilles, both raise a hand

A chilles churned in his clotted thought,
Still undecided. But his friend,
His true guide, Patroclus, caught
At his arm, and shook it. 'Come,
You know what's best. Just do it.
You must seek out your home.
You are the king's son. Be so.
Find Peleus and Thetis,
Their welcome. Now, just go.
This war's no longer yours.

And I, your life-long friend,
Advise you: forget the cause
Of Troy, of Menelaus,
Of greedy Agamemnon,
Of them who have betrayed us.
I'll stay behind. Your fleet
Shall be at my command.
Pick out the ship most sweet
To your desires. Your horses,
Those that you love and trust,
Take them too, for your courses
Must fly across the land
To keep you safe to Parnassus
And Delphi. There, command,
Cajole, entice the Pythia
To speak encrypted words,
Disguised enlightener.
Follow them as you may.
But now, my dearest friend,
Leave me. This is the darkest day
Of all my life.'

Two men talked the night away.
Star-fade fore-ran the coming day.
Patroclus turned away.
He could not bear to stay.
He sent his friend away.
As night fled from the day
Achilles turned away
His face where hot tears lay.
He did not wipe away
The salty trace. It would stay
Unwashed, long ways away.

He turned down to the bay,
And as he trudged away
He saw the tall masts sway
On waves to carry him away.

Pious Achilles breathed his day-hymn,
Watching bright stars fading one by one,
First in the east, where wolf-grey at the rim
Of the long line of misty Evvia hung.
The dark edge pivoted, and night withdrew,
Pulled back the cloak of stars, and over there,
In front, far off, downhill, beyond the straight, eased through
The change from wolf to dove to pearl, and spare
White vapours rose from mountain-tops to show
The faintest shimmering of lemon-rose,
That deepened minutely to coral glow,
Warmed the thin cloud ascending from the snows,
And lit, blood-red upon the high white edge...
'No, no,' Achilles prayed, blood-sate, replete.
And answering , Apollo burst upon the fringe,
Pricking his sunlight round Achilles' feet
Fingered with shadows from the highest top.
Even as the god climbed and sunglow grew,
Achilles quickened, trod the steep path's drop
Down to the ships, his fleet.
                                         He needs a crew,
A vessel, stores, and secrecy for shipping
North to his new life. Let them think him cowed,
Humiliated. Past watch-guards, quipping,
Mockingly, may he still be allowed
To manage his own ships, sailing wifeless?
His sore heart boils; he clamps its hot ferment;
He passes quietly, gloating in smugness;

He'll use this unkind wind Artemis sent.

Descending to the sea, to Evvia's shade,
His head jerked as the sunbright left his eyes.
His sandals lapped by wavelets, now he'll wade
Knee-deep. thigh-deep, waist-deep...
                                         Apollo denies...
He, the compassing god of glory and swift death,
Shadowed Achilles wading by the shore. The god's breath
Spoke in the mortal mind, 'My quivering arrow cried
To pierce your heel. Defray your death to me denied.
Placate Artemis and Apollo, us, who now hold
Your life in ransom. Your bride's dead. Come, man, be bold.'
Achilles stared to seek the dazzle of the sun:
'Brother Apollo, Sister Artemis,
Pardon my negligence. My new life's begun.'

His duty's not yet done. A man's new life
Demands a man's new vows, a sacrifice.
What has he left to give? No fleet, no wife.
What strips him bare, makes poor, what will entice
Protection from the necessary god?
He spreads his hands on the grey, wrinkling wave,
Touches and sees his waist-pouch, dangling pod
Of marriage gifts for her he could not save.
Quick, quick, undoes the toggle, drawing forth
The marvellous golden neckband fashioned
For Iphigeneia, for her whose worth
Her father bet to bribe Artemis' bond.
Achilles bends his back, sweeps high his arm
Behind his shoulder, till the jewel licks
The sea's flat surface, stilled in eerie calm,
And forwards in a soaring arc that flicks
Sea-drops and light-drops, gold-drops up above

To meet the now re-dawning sun, and curves
Sweetly to the waiting sea. releases with love
The sacrifice. Gods grant as it deserves.
'Apollo, Artemis, gods of my death,
A second gift from me, my diadem,
My royal headband, vowed with new-drawn breath,
Golden with images of horse-proud men;
And my last treasure, earrings for my bride:
Artemis riding stags, with weapons raised.
Raise still your wild winds gainst that king who lied.
So grant my northward sailing, and be praised.'
Hurled by voice and arm, gifts to the distant east
Flew from his spreadled fingers as he plunged
Deep in the lustral water. He's released.
Artemis grants him winds, his debt expunged.

His head, anadyomenos, dazzled
And dazzling in Apollo's second rise
Over Evvia's prickling peaks encastled,
Shakes water from his eyes, his hair, and sighs.
Now would he sleep for hours; but seeks his ship,
Padding the shore-line's foam. His eyes, upcast,
Spy Patroclus, steadfast, who'd thought to slip
A warning to the crew: 'Crisis is past.
Prepare the ship; Achilles will escape.
He heads for home; he'll travel overland,
But on this lively wind, first rounds the cape.'
Patroclus, Achilles, both raise a hand.

His ship's awake; the night-watch broke its fast;
Ropes and pulleys rattle; rowlocks oiled
Turn smoothly; men appear to step the mast,
Eager to start the trip for which they've toiled.
They greet their prince with shouts. Achilles nods,

Steps on the foot-board, hauls the rope, beckons
His helmsman and his oarsmen; pleads gods'
Instructions to sail north for home. Reckons
The southerly winds will carry them a stade
Before north winds awake. Then they'll use eddies
Swirling off the other coast. Each long blade
Dipping and pulling, each man now steadies
His shoulders to the rhythm that his sculpted arms
Dictate under the helmsman's gestured count.

Who saw this outbound ship? Nothing alarms
The Greeks. Would even Achilles dare discount
The Trojan enterprise as less to him
Than pride and honour? They will soon regret
The folly of the insult, face the grim
Void in midst their ranks, and no-one to offset.

Landfall

At sunset he wakes in the plunging prow

A chilles, watchful both ways at one time,
Checks for Greek ships, (sleep has deserted him),
And follows too the helmsman's searching gaze
Across the lines of breakers, rock-pricked ways
And shoals that grab the oars; avoid the weed
Glows purple down below; and now make speed
To calmer water.
                    No Greek ships to beware.
He inhales deep, releases the pent air,
Vaguely aware of his loosening limbs.

When was he last at ease? His head swims;
Sleep and exhaustion swamp him. He lets go.

At sunset he wakes in the plunging prow.
An oarsman brings him bread and warm, weak wine.
How long since he last ate? *Was it when
Patroclus...* His mind skids sideways... *Don't drift.
Watch the bleak coast.* Unbroken shadowed cliff
Looms, spiked black-green with needles at its foot.
The wind is with them. Still there's no pursuit,
Nor cove nor harbour, and each craggy cleft
Bars entry. Pass that last headland on the left,
Steer where the lingering light of the late sun
Glints on the sea beyond. The day's near done.
The helmsman acts, sees where the water's froth
Swirls and cavorts like beans in boiling broth,
Swings with the eddy's curl to ease his men,
And turns the sturdy ship to shore again.

A sandy beach, some pines, a cave, driftwood.
They haul and secure the ropes. Cook evening food
In hearths they build from the beach's boulders.
Eat, sleeping sprawl, ease their creaking shoulders.

Achilles takes the watch, talks to the swinging moon
Crossing the paths of stars; hears soft a tune
Nowhere and somewhere, numinous in air.
Prays to Apollo, Artemis, to share
The inland journey to the Pythia's cell.
He's heard her words are strange, and hard to tell
Exactly what she means. The music winds
Into a melody he knows. He finds
A cradle comfort, warm and loving charm.
The pipe tune fades; the dawn shows east; he's calm.

He steps round quietly all the sleeping men,
Touches the helmsman on the hand, and then
Takes leave. 'Look, Friend, the wind blows from the north.
Easy before the breeze, if you think worth
The troublesome trip to Troy. Patroclus
Would be glad to know my mind. He's anxious
For my future. I know he'll understand
Why I go this way to travel overland.
The gods be with you. Here come my horses,
My company now: my divine Xanthus,
Pedasus, Balius. They do not lie.
They'll see me safe; what Greek kings would deny.

Lakes

Three days they amble, men or gods divine

Great, blond Xanthus leads the horses to the man
Scanning the ground behind the shallow beach:
Sand and brown weed, hopping with flies and rotten
Fish bones, gulls and boulders at back, that reach
And merge into an easy, grassy slope.
And there are paths. Then there'll be men or goats,
Or maybe both. If so, then there is hope
Of milk and meat. He eyes the spray that floats
Higher, halfway across the rising scarp:
A line of springs and little darting streams

Rainbowed by morning light, clear, white and sharp,
That wakes the colours won from mineral seams:
Gaudy rich gold, bright rust and emerald,
Lemon and black streak the rock, recovered
From water flowing deep through courses walled
With jet, and noisy with the flooding river.

Achilles' horses graze. Himself climbs swiftly
To the pass, and at the top looks backward
To his Myrmidons below, now deftly
Setting the sails for their return on board.
Resolute, turns his back to the rising sun
Which throws his shadow far down on the slope.

A lake; a wary watcher sees him come;
Defensive, stands to see Achilles lope
Long-legged, followed by horses, man alone.
The sheep scatter and huddle. Still on edge,
Their shepherd brandishes cudgel and stone,
And hears the stranger shouting from a ledge:
He comes in peace, no pirate he, spreads wide
His hands to show no weapons, he's not armed.
Asks some milk, would like to rest, leads aside
The horses to crop and roll; there's no harm.
The shepherd's still alert: that foreign voice
And who comes from the sea? Out of the sun?
Can this man be a god? The safest choice
Will be to treat him well. 'Welcome, my son.'
The two men talk awhile. Rolled in his cloak
Achilles soundly sleeps the noon away.
The shepherd wonders and worries: *poor folk*
Don't meet the gods; so why did this one stray
Down by my lake?
                    Come, man, act with due care,

Send him onwards with food; send him to meet
Neighbouring shepherds; serve this god-man fair,
And give godwillingly what he'll entreat.

Horses and mounted man depart, 'God speed.'
They halt where there is grass, a hut to lodge.
Apollo prospers the hosts with all they need:
Sends twin and triplet lambs, and keeps wolf-watch.

They splash the reedy edges of the lake:
No river in, none out, yet it stays clear
And fresh to drink; no marsh or fenny brake
To stink the air. Maybe a nymph lives here.
Three days they amble, men or gods divine,
Past low white cliffs and tiny villages.
Strange birds are there, stalking the water-line
With beaks as long as arrows. The sedges
Ring and hum and squawk with agitated flocks
Twittering their strange disturbances.
Achilles wanders and wonders. Rough white rocks
Flicker and wink with quick, bright, secret glances.

Once more they climb. The western bank is steep.
Above, the ridge is like a city's walls
Without defenders, only shepherds to keep
The double watch to east and west. He calls.
No echo answers. Over and beyond,
There is another lake lies broad between
Gentle hillsides, another shallow pond
Rocking with small, flat boats, busy and clean.
Bright flowers like drinking cups float, undulate
Sun discs on its surface; turquoise birds dip
And emerge, beaks fish-full. Sheep-dogs await
The meaning whistle from the shepherd's lip.

Achilles, dreaming, passes through this dream,
Awake and half asleep, moulding his thoughts
Of past and future to a cogent scheme
For his new way of life, and all the fraught
Activity of kings and anxious wars
Into a new-shaped world and a new mind
That somehow keeps the anger, when it roars,
Under control; and learns how to be kind.
'Oh, Patroclus, my Patro, teach me now
Your kindness and your patience.'
                                        Another hill;
Mounted man and horses climb. Past its brow
Another lake spreads on an open plain. Still
Riverless, it reflects the sky's bright blue
In grassland bleached to whiteness by its rocks.
The horses canter briskly, splashing through.
Achilles watches flying cranes in flocks.

Brooding

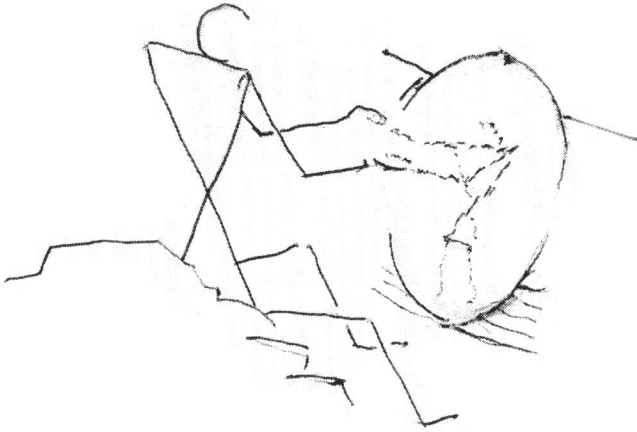

In its glowing mirror... his friend

C ranes, they know their journey's end; so what is mine?
Animals their burrow, so where is mine?
I struggle through the tangles of my thought,
The briars that my cruel behaviour wrought
To trip my feet. I broke up lives in blood;
I swore and raged, and when my kind friend stood
In front to calm me, I struck him aside.
And still he offered help, and still he cried,
'Achilles, think of friendship, think of love.'
Oh, Patroclus, your friendship you did prove:

Gave me as gift the sacrifice of friendship.
Teach me your kindness. Do not let life strip
That gift away. I will learn to be kind,
And with your help, I'll dominate my mind.

His horses have more strength than earth-bred horse,
But even they at sunset halt their course:
Herbs for the horses, lamb's meat for the man.

Colder than when his journey first began,
The wind blows steady on the open ground.
For Achilles, the horses now surround
His body, chilled by gusts swept from the north
Where frozen Parnassus drives fiercely forth
Its icy air. Achilles, warmed and snug
Between his horses, sleeps as with a drug.
Dreams come, rattling his mind, deeds from his past
Rise up: he can't escape; his struggles last
Until his horses nudge him into dawn.
The blue, dim light calms him; a sound comes borne:
A god fingering the strings of the air;
That same tune, numinous, which he heard there
Down on the beach. He washes in the dew,
Picks herbs, strikes sparks to warm a mountain brew.

Today's a day for thinking. He'll not ride,
But walk, unravel pain close there beside
His steady horses. Even so, he stumbles,
Guides his footsteps by their hooves, and fumbles
Through the midden of his past, to seek
What he now needs to conquer, purge the bleak
Appalling deeds that he has done. The blame
Lies where?
                    'My mother? No, hers was the shame

Of marriage to a mortal. She worked in love
For me, to give me more. And who would shove
The burden of a wilful goddess wife
On to poor Peleus? He's lived for all his life
In competition which he cannot match;
Gave me my godly horses, so I'll snatch
Accusation back from him. There's a gift
Worth gratitude.
                                    Who now is left
To bear the weight of my bad deeds? Oh, gods,
Would that I could blame you. You set the odds,
But I still rolled the dice.
                                    Companions
Of the war? Yes, we all fought, but not a one
Rejoiced, like me, at all the pain he caused,
At all the heaps of death. I never paused
In my excess. But the next day, bitter
My tongue, burning dry my eyes, nor fitter
Was my mind, outhollowed like a cave
And filled with black blood, flowing like a wave
From wounds and gashes, while the piteous cry
Of victims still rose up from Acheron.
                                             And I
Collapse into the arms of Patroclus.
Dear gods, how could he love me? Between us
There was no common ground: I was roughness,
Brute maleness. He fought, yes, but tenderness
Suffused his heart, and spread to all his deeds.

Friendship must be my guide. To others' needs
I'll turn my path, and steer my mind
Into the way he taught, learn to be kind.'

That day, the wind blew warmer from the west.

They rested with a goat-flock, drank their best
And sweetest milk. Achilles saw their hooves,
Tiny and neat, jump light across the grooves
Of rock; wished too that his feet left no mark,
Like theirs; that he could pass without the dark
Portentous shadow following behind.
He trudged on, brooding, as the sun declined,
On other things: the copper-coloured sunsets
Of the Trojan shore, heat and salt sweat,
Men's comradeship, his tall, high-polished shield...
Now, in its glowing mirror, sees revealed
In form and face, his friend, stretching a hand
Out to clasp his. He scarce dares to extend
His own; closes his eyes, and feels the warmth
Of well-known fingers, feels their loving strength.
And smiles. The grief he's felt since Aulis
Drops away. His friend's reflection brings him peace.

Walking with a God

Thigh-deep in gold-white wool, Achilles walked

A s day chills into dusk, the horses graze
   And find warm shelter. A violet haze
Fills the mountain's caverns, moulds its ribs stark,
Still glimmering with faded evening light.
Small animals squeal frantic in their fright,
And scuttle to the safety of the dark.
Tired Achilles eases his bones to stand
And think, a dish of half- warmed meat in hand,
Of the hard road his mind has passed along.
He knows his change of heart but just begun;

He knows both deeds and thoughts must be undone;
Remake himself, and set to right the wrong.
His horses circle him. How warm their flanks.
Perhaps he'll not sleep, muse and offer thanks
For love and Patroclus, and gently drowse
In memory of love and their shared life,
Seek his help to dampen down the strife
That moodiness and stubborn will arouse.

His horses wake him early, snuff their soft noise
Into his ears. Through grey dusk one voice
Pipes, as the earliest, twittering bird
Summons the dawn. Behind the mountain mass
Barely a hint, a smudge, shows at the pass.
Apollo waits until the voice is heard.
The notch of grey behind the mountain fills
Imperceptibly. The shy bird trills,
And light swells gold, and overflows the col
To flush the nearer side. Achilles glories
In its dazzle. He's heard famous stories,
Awaits the god, expectant on a knoll.
He shuts his eyes, bows his head, says a prayer.
His horses crowd behind, they too aware
This is a moment of creation; this
Is when their man changes from a being
Of death to one whose eyes are bright with seeing
Life's joy, and with remembering its bliss.
Achilles looks again, sees with surprise
A second sun approaching. Its small size
Marks it a youth, sun radiance in his hair,
And followed by a hustling, baaing flock,
Whose fleeces glint with white and gold: such stock
As nibbles only on gods' pastures rare.

'Ho, Stranger, splendid horses at your heels.'
His bright hair dazzles, and all else conceals.
'Ho, Shepherd, did you rise as second sun?
This is the second double dawn I've seen.
A god brought me the first. Has Phoebus been
Called up twice by birdsong? Are you that one?'
The Sun-boy laughed. 'Come, sit and eat with me.
You're hungry. You'll find I've food that will agree
Your taste.' Achilles sat. Unparalleled,
This food, gift of the sun. Vigour filled up
His body, light as air; drank from a cup
Of oakwood; felt his dragging woe dispelled.
The shepherd stood. His flock moved off ahead
Around Achilles' feet; the horses spread
Out to the edges of the group as wolf-watch
With the dogs. Achilles knew the honour.
Dare he speak now to this boy? Donor
Of such a gift? The shepherd smiled a twitch.
Thigh-deep in gold-white wool, Achilles walked.
Cloaked in a gold-white fleece, the sun-boy talked.
'These are Apollo's shrines along the road.
There they make music. Do you hear it now?'
The sheep-bells mingled tinkling with the low
Meadow sounds, bees, grasses, in a softer mode.
Achilles hesitates, 'I know this tune.
I heard it by the water, and after, soon,
Splashing through the lake, wind plucking the lyre,
The sweet same tune accompanied my thought
Of bitter things, and the new life I sought;
Offered me strength, to follow my desire.'
Looking full at the boy, 'What does it mean?
Young man, I think you're wiser than you seem.'
The boy's eyes glittered brighter than his hair.

A god grew from the boy, freeing his limbs,
And from a sanctuary, pious hymns
Rang out. The mountain sang into the air.

'It is a time when gods and heroes meet on mountain paths.
If you're no hero, I'm no god. But still perhaps
We'll have a conversation.
This is my mountain, Parnassus.
Which is yours? I think your horses have a mountain home.'
'Pelion is mine, and theirs,
Where I put on a beard, and grew from youth to man,
Poseidon's gift to my father, then my father's gift to me,
                                        these horses.
Terrible in battle, tender as a nurse to me.'
'Tell me your story, Hero.'

Achilles told his story, childhood and youth;
Hesitated sometimes, reluctant with the truth,
But told it straight, confessed his savage deeds,
Forced out those episodes that caused him shame.
But when he came to say Patroclus' name
Choked on his tears: the friend who'd sown the seeds
From which his new life sprang. Apollo lent
A quiet murmur, gave encouragement:
'And so... ah, then... he did? Well done, my friend.
Your anger must wear out.' To cleanse his brain,
The hero must tell all, even the latest stain
Of Iphigeneia's death, her dreadful end.
They stop to rest, visit a little shrine,
Stone-built, an altar, and a cup of wine
Beneath an oak-tree, water at its feet.
Achilles sits, thinking a little while
Of Patroclus. The god smiles half a smile:
Let him have memory, let it be sweet.

'Come man, you smell the dew upon the air.
My sheep seek shelter from this hillside where
The westward curving sun bronzes their bells,
Jangling with sharp impatience for their rest.'
The god halts at a fork. 'Leave me. It's best.
The sun drops to the sea. You'll find small dells
Where you can sleep, your horses keep their watch.
We'll meet again.' He turns. The crimson sun-rays catch
His hair. His white sheep melt into the whiter mists.
Purple cloud-shadows swirl around his hips.
He vanishes into the sun that slips
Behind the earth. Only his shadow still persists.

Warmed by a little fire, Achilles dreams,
Fixing Parnassus' peak, where the high beams
Of westering sun irradiate the snow.
Up where the air's still bright, a bird soars regal,
Not vulture of the flesh-fields, but an eagle
Piercing the air to scan the pass below.
Bird and man lock eyes. Recognition grows:
Great god and hero; awed. Achilles bows.
Clouds, noctilucent in the sky, glow green,
And part about recumbent Artemis,
Her silver crescent tender as a kiss
Brushed on the pearly surface of a dream.
Knees locked, heads low, Achilles' horses doze,
Ears pricked for danger. Round about them goes
The nightly tragedy of small lives lost.
Artemis dips below the earth's dark line,
Joining her brother's feast of meat and wine
At tables set by their paternal host.

The Horses

A little hill... a sliding wave of flowing, solid scree

The earth judders.
　Achilles shudders
In his late sleep.
　　　　　No horror in his dreams.
Stars wink in the inky sky. Calm, it seems.
But he wakes alert, quickens his muscles
To unknown threats as near him grass rustles.
He rolls away, and now sees by his face
His careful horses, crowding in his space,
And nudging him softly with their hooves

Out of their way. Obedient, he moves.
Their whiskered muzzles whisper in his ear
That they have knowledge not for him to hear.
He scrambles to his feet, and goes before,
Pushed by their urgent shoulders. They know more,
Encourage his steps, a trot, a run,
His fastest speed. Today it's not the sun
They wait for; feel instead, a frightened sense
Of earth's collapse. In horrified suspense
They reach a little hill, there halt and breathe.
The hump of stone their refuge or their death.
Shocks tingle in their feet, the bushes sway.
And in among the first signs of the day
Disturbance in the trembling earth and air
As birds fly raucous. Animals appear
And run, more fearful of their crumbling holes
Than of the crows or kestrels or the owls.

Zeus thunders in the air, Poseidon in the earth.
Man and horses stagger, cliffs crack open in the birth
Of gullies loosing rocks which flow in a cascade
Pouring from all sides, relentless in a sliding wave
Of flowing, solid, tumbling, shattered, grey, white scree,
A slithering avalanche to the mountain's knee.
The mountain's face is gone; the roaring triangle
Of flighted stone slides down itself to mangle
Deep in rubble the little dell of last night's rest.
Achilles, dust-blinded, leans hard on Xanthus' chest.
Coughing and spitting, choking and heaving his lungs,
Tries to clear from his ears the tumult that still drums.
Hears the rasping of his horse's breath, lifts his head,
And sees, above the devastated dell, all dead,
The triangle of dust that fills the triangle of sky,

And mounting, mingles grey with snow-dust, flying high,
Illuminated by the new day, sparkling white,
Thrown by the shaking earth into the sun's clear light.

The three great horses crowd Achilles' flank.
He fondles them, wondering how to thank
Their duty and their love. What do horses need?.
Green pasture, gentle care, sweet water, feed.
He pauses on a sigh.
                              Where did he come from,
That handsome figure, followed by his sheep?
'Sir, out of all this rock, how did you come?'
'Rock is no obstacle. You think I creep
Through holes and crevices? I am your thought.
I came because you need to give a gift.
What shall it be?'
                              Achilles pauses, caught
By the idea's majesty. No more bereft
Of answers, beckons the great animals.
'My lord Apollo, to you I present
Xanthus, Pedasus and Balius, ideals
Of prowess and divinity. Consent,
Permit, that serving me, they serve you too.'
Graceful as fillies, noble as the god,
The horses step, extend their necks, and bow.
Apollo, radiant, smiles and throws a wad
Of wool, a riding cloth of golden fleece
On Xanthus' back, silver for Balius, pearl
For Pedasus. The air stills in sudden peace.

'Come, breakfast, man.' And in the woolly swirl
Of horns and legs and tails, god and man hear
A distant rumble, see a wisp of dust.
'Ah, there he goes, my father, gone from here.

I supped with him last night. He values trust,
Saw you at dusk, and marked your reverence.
Eat up. We have a journey. Shall we ride?'

The Three Ways

Thebes, Daulis, Delphi... even simple truths tell lies

G ently, skirting the cliffs, the path declines,
Kind underfoot, while in the mountain's pleats
There's evidence of clean rock, new ravines
That opened in the dawn. Crowding, their bleats
And bells merging to a rhythm and a tune
Achilles heard before, Apollo's flock trots
And browses as it goes. The man looks down,
Lulled by the undulating, woolly knots
To a half-sleep. The whispering music
Comes and goes. Old memories, new visions

Weave through the phrases, broider fantasies,
Plans, reform, renown, peace, reputation.

He rides along, sheep pace, horse pace, thought pace;
Remembers what Apollo said to him,
'I am your thought.' Could he, a man, embrace
The god within his mind, fill to the brim
His small mortality with a god's ideas?
It is a fearful thought. If he mistake
His nature for the god's, what then? He peers
Aghast at dreadful actions he might take.

Apollo leans across, touches his hand.
'Look about you. Come, join me at that sign.'
Achilles leaves the horses, goes to stand
At a junction where three ways mark the line
Between three hillocks into a far-off mist.
No eagle in the sky, no vultures swooping:
Still, he ducks his head, hears wings that hissed,
But cast no flying shadow; saw drooping
The pleasant flowers, the seeded grass; shivers
As with the onset of a dreadful curse.
Thebes, Daulis, Delphi. The question quivers:
'What horror do I feel? This is far worse
Than anything I have known. I need courage
To brace myself against myself. That's a thing
I have not had to learn: just men and carnage.
I shall need courage against myself within.'

Now, trotting lightly, dances, nearly flies,
A young man comes to join them, quick smile, sly.
'Welcome, cousin.'
                          'Cousin? Brother?'
                                        Grey eyes

Smirk, amused. Truth and lies slip equally
From that laughing mouth. 'Hermes, Achilles
Who serves me goes to Delphi. Needs advice
Concerning what he'll hear, how he should please
The prophetess, persuade her and entice
From enigmatic words a simple truth.'
'Ah, even simple truths tell lies. Once was,
Is now, will be, perchance, a simple truth
May drive a simple man calamitous
To a future not as he intended.'
'Who is he? Was he?'
                                        'Well, a wise man knows
That he is any man. Let any man be minded
That he is author of all ill he sows;
But he must share the authorship of good,
A heavier burden altogether.
That's my message. Now, Brother, here is food
To fit this man for trials that he must weather.'

Achilles shares the meal of these two gods,
Bemused at how he's stumbled into this.

'Brother, Cousin, farewell.' Achilles nods
As they clasp hands, attentive lest he miss
An instant of the scene. Hermes is gone,
Near out of sight. His sandals raise no dust.
'How did he get so far? I could not run...'
Apollo, not unkindly, laughs. 'I trust
You do not think you could compete with him,
Oh, swift Achilles. His being's light as air.
Look in your mind, and know how he can run.
He too is thought; he and I, everywhere.'

Leave behind the loitering flies that hover

Where the horses went; leave too this bad place
Shadowed by words and omens, recover
The lovely balance of Apollo's grace.

Apollo sees Achilles deep in thought:
Impossible to foresee man's fate and doom;
A man alone wreaks ill, needs friends for aught
Of good; friends are the answer, not the gloom
Of mourning for dead heroes. I will live.
'Apollo, I am ready. Shall we walk?'

Almost arm in arm, hero attentive,
Opens his spirit to Apollo's talk:
He tells of all the arts, their uses
For sweet persuasion and diplomacy,
Of ways to strength without war's cruel abuses,
Of friendship and its gentle potency.
'But there are men...'
                            'Yes, there are men who know
Nothing but power by war. You're not of them.
Your ears are tuned to music of Apollo now.
You hear and sing my songs; you speak my poems.
The arts of peace, the stories of great men
That teach the lessons of the past. Think well
The dangerous story of him, who then,
Or when, or sometime will act to propel
An unknown, unsought future on himself.'

The mountain path smoothes and widens
To where the lipped slope terminates, a shelf
To stand and part before the end still hidden.
Down there, in front, lies the broad Delphic valley;
Shrine and sanctuary on their terrace
Stepped into the hill, and flanked equally

Both sides by Parnassus' arms' safe embrace.
'My Pythoness is there, who speaks my words,
Listens to whispers from the fumy hole,
But doesn't understand what she has heard.
She's just a voice; messenger is her role.
I won't descend. If I went down, my priests
Would not know what to do. Pilgrims have needs
More pressing than preparing mighty feasts
For me. You'll hear them chant. Join with their creeds,
And sing the airy music from your head.
Evening has come. The sun draws me away
To where the Muses have spread out my bed.
We'll meet next on your acclamation day.'

The hero and the god stood side by side,
Illumined at the high brow of the col.
Achilles bowed his head. He would not hide
His tears: 'My friend in honour.' That was all.
Apollo too, 'Hero, my honoured friend;'
Turned, was engulfed behind the shadowed rock,
Melted into the sunset's crimson end,
Followed by dogs at heel and crimson flock.

Resolute now,
Achilles leads his horses down the hill
Into the vale of Delphi.
Shivers beneath his cloak.
It's chill.

Delphi

'Apollo said you might.' 'Apollo says you may.'

'**A**re they gods? Are they horses? Are they men?
On the pass.
They are huge, just outlines..
How many? Two, no, just one... three horses.'

Wonder and worry halt the slow processional prayers.
Pilgrims and priests shuffle and shield their eyes.
The altar child, Apollo's servant, dares
To speak aloud in innocence what age denies.
'I saw. There was a god here at the newborn moon.
He disappeared at sunset with a girl,

The day before the temple roof fell down.
I knew at once; my thoughts were in a swirl.'

Nearly dark in the valley, long shadows encroach
On the sacred ground. Achilles' horses
Guide him down the slope, steadily approach
The foot of the looming walls. Achilles pauses.
'We'll spend the night here. Succulent grass and water
For you. My god-given meal still satisfies.'
Artemis' throne has set; Zeus's daughter
Leaves the stars to glitter silver where the temple lies.

Wrapped in his cloak, Achilles sleeps, while careful dogs
On temple guard sniff round his peaceful couch.
The friendly gurgling of the courting frogs
Makes no disturbance.
                              He wakes at day's first touch.
Birds have supplanted frogs. Their intricate song-lines
Fill his ears. His own song winds in quietly:
'Flutes of the air,
Lyres of the grass,
Drums of my horses' hooves.
Voices of my gods.'

Children wake early. Running down the slope,
The temple child with breakfast in an envelope
Of leaves, shouts that she knows that holy song.
'You've met the god that haunts here. All along,
Since first I saw him, I've known. I've waited
For you to come. Some breakfast? Cheese grated,
And a little meat, the old priest's oil and bread.'
Achilles, entranced, lets himself be fed.
While they eat, the child still babbles. 'Pilgrims,
They come here all the time. They chant some hymns,

And then the priest sets them to clear rubble
That clogs the spring. Sometimes they make trouble.
But the priest says, 'Work together, doing good.
That's wisdom of the world.' And so they should.
And so the Pythia teaches. They learn twice.
And some, perhaps, act by their good advice.'
'Will you become the Pythia?'
                              'Not until
I am a woman; learn how to be still,
To sit upon the tripod, hide what I see
In mazy words. But here, for you and me,
Apollo's thoughts pass from my head to yours
In flowing waves, as our Castalian spring pours
Godbright from the earth.'
                           A priest comes running.
'Child, go to your tasks.' With priestly cunning
Greets the stranger, 'Our latest pilgrim, Sir.
We'll find you lodgings. Sell you gifts to offer
To the Pythoness. You'll not mind some work?'
Achilles claims the ground for bed; won't shirk
From any task they set him; is not able
To purchase gifts. 'But please, find a stable
Or frisky meadow for my great horses.'
The three had listened to the girl-child,
Closely. She stroked their muzzles, fearless, mild,
Intent. They knew the truth of all her words.

But the priest seems wary. Where are the herds
That these great creatures spring from? And those rugs,
Or fleeces, saddle-cloths. Cautious, he tugs,
Embarrassed, at his beard. 'Perhaps you should
Yourself find them a place.' There where they stood
The grass and herbs and flowers grew lush. 'They chose

To drink where, dark from the rock, the bright spring flows.'
Achilles smoothed his hand down Xanthus' flank.
The horses understood, bent heads, and drank.

Led by the priest towards the tumbled stones
He watched the struggling pilgrims. Each atones
For some remembered misdeed, in this place
To clean the stain, emerge without its trace.
He joins a gang; shoves stones beneath to wedge
The column they are raising on its edge;
Winds ropes to bind; digs holes to settle in
The base of others; grimes knees, and bruises skin.
Apollo in my thought, in you I trust.
And hoists each block up with a mighty thrust.
Exhausts by nightfall all his human strength,
Stumbles with others to the huts. Full length
Spreads weary on the ground, to share
The frugal pilgrim meal, and then to care
For his three loyal horses, rested, pleased
To see him back, drained by the work, but eased.
Sings with the dawn Apollo's tune, and treads
Daily to the ruins. They toil, they seek their beds,
Until the temple's all rebuilt.
                                        Then, one day,
His horses have moved on. He finds where they stray
Along the mountain's edge, by Pythia's cell,
Where she sits on her stool, trying to tell
The hidden truth to pilgrims in their need:
What actions, good or bad, fate has decreed.

The cavern hides black behind a curtain
Of spindly spears of rock, hung uncertain,
Moss-decked and fragile, pendant from its gape.
Within, the Pythia gasps and moans. *Escape,*

Is all Achilles thinks. *This aweful place.*
This suffering seer. In god's name, how find grace,
Within such pain, out of such agony?
Then, swelling on his ear, the harmony
Of his own songs, his own god-given melody,
The flutes and lyres, trust in theonomy,
And chorus from the pilgrims' psalmody
Ringing high from the cliffs in euphony
Knit by the echoes from the cavern's deeps,
Where bound by a god's fierce will, the Pythia weeps.

Weeping too, Achilles ducks low beneath
The dripping spikes of rock in the foul breath
Of choking fumes, and grasps the Pythia's stool.
Now he's inside, he feels how damp and cool
The air is. Odd little sparks of daylight
Glint on the prophet's head, reveal the bright
Moist drops that scatter in her hair like coins
Of precious metal. Her voice, hoarse, harshly enjoins,
'Don't speak. I know you. You have communion
With the god I serve, a tighter union
Than ever I shall. He told you what to do.
I tell you where. Cross water. And there for you
Wait people who are your birthright, willing,
Wanting, longing. Now struggling and spilling
Blood and brains against hostility. Find them.'
The bundle of her body droops, collapses.
He steps back. The priest comes. Bare elapses
The time for her to fall down to the ground,
He's caught her up. Achilles scrambles
Backwards out. Frightened, sorts over the shambles
In his mind. Looks for his horses; comfort
In their solid flanks, though he knows he ought

To be their guardian, not they his. Xanthus
Carries him to the river's bank; Balius
Scrapes the shining mud into a little pile,
Which Pedasus moulds with his frogged hoof, while
Wrought Achilles breaks a twig to mark the stripes
On the small figure. Carefully he wipes
Clear his hands of the holy clay. His prints
Testify to his presence, humble hints
Forever in the statue that his fingers
Shaped this gift, where his devotion lingers.

Supperless, he sleeps, wakes up with the birds
Chilled, but not cold; watches the quiet shepherds
Leading their flocks to temple and terrace;
Wonders what he feels: anguish or solace?
Decides, this simple, half-god man, on breakfast.

The child sits quiet on the step. As he goes past,
'I kept you this,' and opens up her leaves
Which wrap an altar's honey-cake. She heaves
A sigh, content, 'Apollo said you might.'
Tears in his eyes, Achilles takes a bite.
It is the same sustaining, god-made food
As all those other meals. 'Thanks. This is good.'
Breaks off a piece. 'Apollo says you may.'
The child, solemn, takes, eats and looks away.
'Yes, godman, I do know how hard her life;
The dizziness, the choking, inner strife
To put into some order those few scraps
Apollo will allow, see how he wraps
His knowledge up in mystery. The priest fails
To see silver in her hair; just snaky scales.
Look, I have silver hair.' And stands beside
Blond Xanthus; two silvers blend and hide

One in the other.
     'It is a frightening trade.'
'Achilles, yes, I know. And I'm afraid.'
'Apollo bless you, child. Your time must come.'

The sun lifts over the mountain. The busy hum
Of insects rhythms the pilgrims' morning song
In worship near the altar. He's brought along
His little votive statue, lays it there
Among the others at the altar's stair.
He must make his way to water, say goodbye
To the priests. He asks after Thessaly,
Its king and queen. They tell him Peleus has gone,
Returned to Aegina, left them alone with theft,
Disorder, squabbling princelings. Now he must go
To find his father's island, and to grow
To his new role. Apollo's priests bestow
Their blessing. 'Follow the sunset to the shore.'
Apollo's child waves from the temple's door.

He's resolute as he descends: he won't look back.
The slope is easy, but he needs to pick his way
Among the rocks, bruising the leaves of pungent plants,
Moving within the clouds of bees, furry and black,
And sensing more than seeing how the goat path lay
Down to the valley where the mountains rose aslant.

Those are the last hills before the sea, not as tall
As Parnassus, but still he'll take the low, soft route,
Striding easily where the path smells of camomile.
Achilles slaps his horses' sides, watches them all
Rambling through the myrtle and the tiny scarlet fruit
Of early strawberries. Thinks of Apollo's smile.

Sea Way

They tell something of their life or journey

They round the mountain's shoulder; level ground
spreads out
Down to the sea: olive groves, vineyards, little fields. Hands wave
In greeting. These men are more used to visitors
Than those above the pass to Delphi; there's no doubt
That here he'll find some boat to cross the sea, some brave
Adventurer who'll carry him, horses and stores
To land near Corinth, find a way to cross the neck
To the Aegean Gulf.
                    He and his horses find

A sheltered bay beyond the port. He stalks the beach
With patience, spears some fish. On a boat's fore-deck
He hails a boy. 'Come, eat with me.' 'Sir, that is kind.
My father too. We'll bring some food to share with each,'

While the fish sizzle on the heated rocks, they tell
Something of their life, or journey. Widowed, orphaned,
Would man and boy agree to travel through the gulf?
Horses and hero, Apollo's wind and kindly swell?
Achilles prays, and guarantees safe passage to the land
Of Corinth, protection from the pirate sea-wolf.
He's sailed before, will work his way, catch and sell fish.
Tempted, the man's unsure, so one day at a time
They make their bargain, passage paid through
Each night's fish and work. Apollo satisfies Achilles' wish,
And fills the nets; the man's eyes wide, his pockets brim
With gifts. The boy knows more, hears meaning to construe
Escapes his father's ears.
                                              Achilles divines the lad
Has looked below appearances, has caught half-sight
Of mysteries not yet to be revealed. Could he
Have talents useful to the state, but still tight clad
In inexperience, to be unwrapped, that might
Serve the long future well? What did the god foresee?
Join forces, unions, make friends not enemies.
This boy might be the first. There's more within his mind
Than could be used on fishing boats. Two days to sail;
I'll learn his thoughts, then I'll decide. Our destinies
May well twine in together. These two days may bind
Our kingdom glorious into an historic tale.

Apollo hearkened. The light winds fell. The boat drifted.
The water lay so still that one might see reversed
And count the seven pricked reflections of the Pleiades

In its night-black surface. By day, when sea-mist lifted,
They heard the dolphin's song far off as they conversed,
And sibillations of the flying fish, at ease
Below the father's eye, gentling the tiller's shaft,
Who noted all through the salty days the growing bond
Between the hero (now he knows) and this new youth
Who's blossomed from the simple fish-boy at his craft;
With heavy heart concedes this lad, of whom he's fond,
Should seek the world, grow to a man in his own truth.

Some later night, sailing by Corinth's northern cliffs,
The youth sits at his father's feet. 'My son, I know.
Yes, you may leave. This man has studied the working
Of your mind. Navigate his court, not coastal skiffs.
He'll show the path and practice best for you to follow,
Find out from your untried heart what lies there lurking.'

Father and son sleep close. At dawn, the older says,
'We've come to shore. It's always at the very edge
One makes decisions. Now or not. Have you yet told
That brave man what you want? The parting of our ways?
Or life with fish, longing for what's lost, while you dredge
Sand from your sandals and sullen tears from dreams gone cold?'

Achilles jumps ashore; his horses spring like gods
From the rocking boat. The youth looks in his father's eye,
Bends, embraces him, follows the beckoning hand.
'My father said that I could come.' Achilles nods.
'Take me where you will for friendship, for my road lies
Where you direct. My actions are at your command.'

The youth's again a boy. He's watched those horses,
Begs a ride. 'If they agree. They choose who mounts them.
But first, a name for you.'
                              'I'll be Apomeros,

"From some place else". Achilles laughs, and so endorses
The name. 'Go, greet the horses. Don't look so solemn.'
He runs to stand in front; stops, and bows. courteous,
Before he slips between their shoulders, cups in pride
His hands below their necks. Muzzles turn to his face,
Whiskers and warm breath. Silver-fleeced Balius kneels,
Invites him up. Nimbly he climbs and sits astride
Where once a god sat. Achilles notes well his grace.
He is my scout and messenger, my truth reveals.

Passing through level fields, they cannot go unnoticed.
The cavalcade draws after it men in small groups.
To some Achilles speaks, some others he ignores.
Is this an army? No, rather, they're men who've missed
The Trojan venture: young farmers, not warrior troops,
Looking for land, a new start, wives on other shores.
Achilles leads his followers to the sea's edge.
He'll not take them yet to Aegina. He must meet
His parents on simpler terms: just Apomeros
And the horses. To the Corinthians, he gives a pledge:
He will return to them, though not command a fleet.
He doesn't sail for conquest, but consensus.

The men make camp, compliant with Achilles' wish.
Man, boy and horses charter a deep-hulled ship
For Aegina, two nights at sea, crossing the deep.
Achilles thinks on Patroclus; the lad pulls fish,
While telling himself stories of his hero's trip
Past lakes, cross land, with gods, until he falls asleep.

Peleus and Thetis

The king and queen watch from the cliff on stools

Rumour spreads ahead: all those fish, unnatural;
The following wind, gentle skies: exceptional;
Gods must have brewed some scheme fantastical
To catch out credulous mortals, delusional;
Fisher and boy still can't believe, irrational.

The rumours reach Corinth, leap through the land,
Carried to Aegina by an impetuous wind,
Where Peleus and Thetis wait and understand.

Each day they climb together to the high cliff-tops,

Through bare, uncultured fields, or flattened crops.
And then, chill silence intervenes, their conversation stops.
First faces, then they turn their backs; what is there left to say?
They walk apart; each one mistrusts the day
When their wild son will reappear in this quiet bay.

She braces herself for cruel recrimination,
Defends herself against the accusation
That she withdrew her love. But there was no cessation
Of love and anguish in her heart: she knew she'd lose
Her son to death; she knew she had to choose
Acceptance of her marriage; she could not refuse
Zeus's command to bear and love a mortal boy.
Thus he remained. No art she could employ
Would outwit death, no substitute would death destroy.
Her dread is losing him while she remains alive,
Alive for ever. No bargain she could drive
Would save her from eternity, let hope survive.
What if he's grown up kind? That might be even worse
Than cruelty. Then nothing could disperse
The grief that floods her heart: his blessing as her curse.
But whom does a goddess pray for help?

Thought he, mere vanity then tempted me to court
The goddess, warning even as she fought
That it would be a lifetime's folly I had bought
Accepting Zeus's challenge to make her my bride:
A son greater than me. A source of pride
To any mortal man. Though Zeus might well decide
His family story weighed against the omen,
I had no such fears. My wife killed children
Until the gods stepped in; then this one was stolen
And sent to play the maid. But she had no defence
When boy resurfaced man from the pretence,

And learnt the trade of arms. But prowess caused offence.
Hero he was at Troy; but spiteful Agamemnon,
Envious, conspired to put him down,
And, as I heard, he fled, set out by ship alone,
Who knew where.
                          Agamemnon's men maraud my shore.
My men have gone to Troy; women grow poor;
No men makes no children. Who is there to ensure
My kingdom will survive?
                          But now this rumour comes,
Past Corinth, over sea, this rumour drums
Achilles on his way; in my ears rumour hums
Its tempting song. What may I dare to understand?
Will he bring strife, further degrade my land?
Kill me, expel his mother, then usurp my wand?
What if he's lost his force, or hides himself in guile,
Undermining with a treacherous smile
My good name, sends me defamed off to exile?
Perhaps he's had wise counsel, or perhaps mapped out
A plan of rescue. Maybe there's no doubt
Nibbling his mind what he can do to bring about
Peace in this sad kingdom.
                          Harmony with my wife
Would start us off well. Living is for life.
She broods Achilles' death; she concentrates on grief.
Sometimes she's here, and sometimes not, while no-one knows
The table where she dines. Her blank face shows
That though she does not age, oldness within her grows.
But whom does an old king pray for help?

The king and queen watch from the cliff on stools.
Can she be kind, now he's grown old? Old fools
Make friends, live by some different set of rules?

One day, a young man climbs up to their seat.
He's tall, he's bright, he bounces on his feet.
Thetis and he each waves a hand to greet
The other. 'Hermes.'
                                        'My cousin.'
                                                        Peleus
Knows that he must wait, patient and courteous
While they play out the ritual; staid and decorous,
The two exchange their family news:
The quarrels of Hera, and Zeus's views;
Which heroes at Troy have died and paid their dues.
At last he asks, 'Achilles? Will he come?
Calm? Or in his usual wild delirium?
And when? How soon? We know where he'll come from.'
'One day, quite soon, the northern summer wind
Will blow him here. But calm or disciplined?
That's to find out.' Mischievous Hermes grinned,
And slipped away, a god to pray for hope.

Aegina

The veteran from Troy knows both horse and man

Hieratic statues they seem, seated, he and she,
Still as mountains before they shake to dust,
Apprehending his anger, not unjust,
Or worse, contempt for what they have allowed to be.

Leant on the ship's prow, Achilles watches eagerly
The north cliff of Aegina's sheltered bay;
Practising, discarding what he might say
In greeting, familiar or formality?

The deep-hulled boat crunches and grinds the pebbly shore.

Thetis and Peleus have not yet stirred;
How cross that gap of years, find the right word?
The horses give voice, prance free and preen their splendour.
Peleus hears the echo of the well-loved sound,
Thetis too hears the voice of the sea-god's gift.
They know Achilles will come soon, and swift
Declare what he intends, whether to heal or wound.

This is a serious moment, meeting of son
With father, meeting of son with mother
On a bright hillside; like any other
Estranged family, trust needs to be won.
Whispered on the wind, they hear Apollo's song.
The tall man, striding between his horses,
Sings it out loud. Peleus, startled, pauses
And knows himself the lesser man, knows it's not wrong,
But as it should be. Thetis stands wondering
At his stature, presence. Last seen a boy,
She still would know him anywhere, weeps with joy,
Whose glory kills her grief, all sadness sundering.

Achilles stoops, 'Now, Apomeros, your tongue must plead
My embassy and tell my tale. Recount
All that you've heard of my adventures. Mount
Balius, carry my message on a noble steed.'

The youth fulfils all courtesies, and is received
With matching grace; declaims Achilles' story:
Gods and shepherds, earthquake, fear, the glory
Of Apollo's friendship; priests; what he has believed
On Aegina to be both duty and his pleasure:
Restoration of order to the kingdom
Of his parents; restoration of freedom
From piracy to the people in full measure.

Achilles approaches, leads the horses to the king,
Who, fondling them, weeps: full restitution
Of Achilles' love. Thetis, with passion,
Embraces him, grief in the instant quite forgetting.

Food, beds, stables, the hospitable house puts forth
Its best. Achilles tells over more details
Of his journey: the Pythia (Thetis pales)
Apollo's holy child, the walks, the horses' worth;
The sacrifice of Iphigeneia; Patroclus,
Whose sacrifice of friendship and of love
Made possible Achilles' quest to prove
Himself a better man; and young Apomeros,
Whose new, poetic skill made with the message
A crack in the chrysalis of his youth;
Made of Achilles' impulse ample proof
That he would be a bard to outlive time's passage.

For a short space, Achilles allows himself to be
An ordinary man. Apomeros teases,
His parents reminisce; him it pleases
To wander in the gardens, plunge into the sea,
To bed a girl. But soon he finds the skins of men
Are thinner than a hero's skin: the cries
Of hungry children, their bleak, fearful eyes;
Farmers, ousted by pirates, looking to him for haven.
When once he surged between violence and apathy,
Now he assumes his right heroic weight
Made mild by this new sense of driving fate,
And what he learned from Patroclus, sweet sympathy.
Blood on my hands in all I did and where I went,
My power was always subject to my weakness.
Now weakness is my power: treat with fairness
Enemies, and make them friends, my anger all outspent.

'Father, your kingdom must be healed. We'll take our horses,
And ride through Aegina across and round
Till the invading pirates have been found;
Persuade them that allies call on more resources.
Father, I do not want to fight. I fear the rage
That beats inside my head when I'm opposed.
War's a trade I'm all too good at. Exposed
To battle, I shall learn to avoid Troy's carnage.
I've passed this journey brooding, fighting for control
Of my mad impulses. I must not break
My vows to Patroclus, Apollo; make
The struggle vain. Reconciliation is my goal.'

The pirates occupy the edges of the land.
The islanders survive in stony villages
High in the hills far from the pillagers
Of corn and nuts and sheep, who wield the threatening brand.
Wives and mothers, abandoned by their men, widowed,
Poor and lonely, plead with Achilles for aid,
Men and children. The pirates may be swayed
By promises of amnesty and land in peace bestowed.

Threading through the island, people follow after
To where they spy the pirates on the coast,
Young, raucous, feasting on stolen fruit and roast.
Apomeros reports their bawdy laughter,
Longing for women, theirs by capture or persuasion.
They've settled for the night. Achilles plans
To leave them helpless. He carefully scans
The number of their ships; plots a conflagration
By sending the local fishermen to burn the hulls,
So to persuade them to capitulate,
Or fight against superior force. Too late
Then, to sail to Piraeus with the screaming gulls.

First, they smell the smoke, burning canvas, oil; consterned
They check their weapons and their shabby tents;
All's safe in camp; the sea-wind blows the scents
Of timber, rigging, pitch and booty: all ships burned.
The young ones seize their weapons, act as though to rush
Against a foe; the older sit, take counsel
To withstand this unexpected peril.
All know they now have little power. And in the hush
That settles on their clamour, they see approaching
Three men and mighty horses. Who are so bold
That they come without an escort?
                                    Now rolled
A monstrous wave, a tumbling sea. Fear encroaching
On their courage, there's only one man left with heart
To act the man. He stands prepared to talk.
The hush extends; the horses at slow walk
Come nearer, nearer. With a sickening start,
The veteran from Troy knows both horse and man.
A backward step, he draws his sword; then shocked,
Sees that the youngest, bonnet neatly cocked,
Rides out alone.
                  Achilles' envoy states the plan:
Pirates surrender weapons; each man swear an oath
To keep the peace; farm or work at their trades;
Marry such widows as willing; not touch maids;
And with conditions, in five years, and if not loth,
Become free citizens of Aegina. Elsewise, fight,
Withstand Achilles' power, experience,
Oppose a half-god, known for his violence.
Apomeros bows, takes his leave. Decide tonight.

The pirates on the seashore pass the night in thought.
Uneven choice. The offer's generous.

To be a bondsman can be onerous.
But fight Achilles? That were death too cheaply bought.

At dawn the veteran trudges, weaponless, up
To the high cliff where stands Aphaia's altar.
Fearful and yet steady, his steps don't falter.
Achilles can be trusted. There he drinks a cup
Of wine to pledge the oath. Then come all the others,
The young ones at the end. They have no trade,
No wish for widows. What makes them afraid
Is growing old as bondsmen, service that smothers
All their spark and spirit. Achilles recognises
Their vigour. He will make them the defence
Of Aegina, training them in battle sense,
And war and valour, men's work no man despises.

They claim, 'We thought you were at Troy.'
                                        'No, no, I left,
Came home to set to rights this harassed realm.
You plagued my father while I wore a helm.
Now we'll have peace; our king a kingdom, not bereft
Of hope for time to come.'
                            The company returns,
Escorting the bondsmen, a bewildered band,
But sizing up the widows and the land:
Each is willing for the fair reward his labour earns.

Restoring the Kingdom

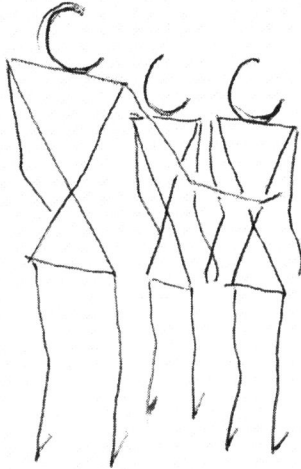

Thetis watches the king grow old, cares for him

Conversion of the pirates is not the end.
The days of making peace to months extend.
Other marauding bands are brought to heel.
Work and acceptance quench desire to steal.
The eager youths take well to discipline.
The marriages for pity's sake begin.

In winter conversations by the fire
King and prince discuss measures they require
To turn the kingdom right way up again.
Men they now have; an army to maintain

The safety of the coast; and come the spring
There will be babies. Aphaia's priests will sing
To celebrate the peace.
                                    In the palace,
His son's support brings Peleus solace.
'Every house has its back yard. Mine is here.'
He strikes his chest. 'Envy of Thetis, fear
Of her contempt; for you, a mix of pride
And fear that you too, half-god, might decide
That Peleus, as father, was not good enough.
Outwards, I put on swagger and high bluff.
But for the kingdom, I could not resolve
The problems. So, let anarchy evolve.'
'Zeus was cruel to force you to this marriage.
He made half-gods, though women seem to manage.
Thetis will watch you aging, long to flee.
But she will stay. Her agony's for me,
That I, like you, will die and she will not,
That she will never meet life's last despot.'

They'll plan new buildings, travel through the isle;
Build up a fleet, fair, just laws compile;
Encourage trading, inland and oversea,
Theatre and music, dance and poetry.

In spring, father and son quarter the land:
Each harbour, ship-yard, bay of rock or sand;
Each temple, tavern, farm-yard and market;
Each quarry, stone-yard, forest and secret
Grove of nymphs and dryads, sacred oak-trees,
Ivies and humming pines, habited by bees.
Their people know them, horses and the men,
But more, they know the people once again.

Aegina is small, a pea-sized kingdom,
No-one visits it, or only seldom.
A man could walk all round it in three days,
Between two moons walk all its inland ways,
Climb all its hills, and still have breath to laugh.
And that is what Achilles finds. He half
Forgets he was a fighter, wonders why
He never looked at trees, or sea or sky,
Or people, before he met Apollo.
Aegina fills up the aching hollow
Of severed feelings and uncertainty
He's had since Aulis. Here his sovereignty
Derives from service and due affection,
Not from brute strength wielded in contention.
Fighting was so simple – he just did it.
Being a king's a struggle without limit.

The island's trade in spring picks up its pace:
Seasoned timber, fish and cheese, and where there's space,
Fine blocks of quarried stone, white as the hills
That built Aphaia's shrine. When evening stills
The bustle, news from Athens, news from Troy,
Where war continues. Ships fast to the buoy,
The captains drink and gossip, air their views.
Of every captain sailed his ship from there
Achilles asks, 'And Patroclus? Don't spare
All that you know.' Sometimes there comes a word,
Sometimes merely a rumour someone heard.
Then news dries up. No-one will meet his gaze.
He knows death's ended Patroclus's days.

Thetis, no less tall, no less young, watches
The king grow old, cares for him, matches
The way she lives to what he undertakes.

In the long twilights, measures their mistakes;
Anger, resentment, longings unfulfilled;
Peleus hot, Thetis stubborn-willed.
'God-like he never was. I knew what gods were:
Gods spring over time, while humans lumber.
I am bewildered by eternity.
Your lives jostle my long eternity.
Dusty mist in the air of eternity;
Dusty deeds in the mist of eternity;
Misty dust round my feet for eternity.
You see? Eternity repeats forever.
Eternity's a garment worn out never.'
Achilles listens, comes to understand
Her treatment of his youth. He takes her hand.
'There is no consolation. He will die.
And when the Fates decide, then so shall I.'

Acclamation

Peleus... holds out the royal treasures.

In other twilights, other conversations,
Pelcus with Achilles shares his visions
Of Aegina to come, his flickering dreams
Of great perfections in grand schemes:
'Perhaps a splendid temple to Aphaia,
High on her cliff, echoing with her prayer;
Perhaps dominion of the Saronic Sea,
Perhaps our stories to eternity.
But no, man is only necessary
To his own time, a mere accessory

To plans of gods for his life's little space.
I to the son of Thetis now give place.
You have outdone me in all things:
Your strength, your beauty, your reputation sings
Of war and peace, diplomacy and friendship.
You are my heir, both by right of kinship
And by worth.
              Tomorrow, I will summon
The people's chiefs, by their will in common
To declare your right. None will disagree.
As king, my son, you will far surpass me.'
'Then, father, are you now so close to death
That you and I must number out each breath?
Then I beg leave to make you one last gift:
My glorious horses, strong, proud, godly swift,
Are yours again, who gave them me in youth.
They have served me with honour and with truth,
Accompanied my path, comforting and warm,
Preserved my life, and shielded me from harm.
Divine beasts, my great pride, again are yours.
Never did and never will fail you in your cause.
Peleus, overwhelmed, holds close his son,
Knowing the merit in the man he has become.

'It's time to call the people hither
To ascertain their choice of heir: whether
They agree the aptness of the man I choose,
Or if he displeases, whether they refuse.'

The king's word spreads to heads of clans and villages
To hear his new intention; to colleges
Of priests, to bring their chaplets, herbs and wine,
So gods and lords and people can combine
To hear and judge their monarch's last decree,

Express their own adherence, offered free.

Thus summoned forth, the elders come to hear
This declaration of the king: 'See here
The man that I propose to be my heir.
Yours is the final word. The law is fair,
Requires from all the people full consent.
Advise me now how well you are content.'
The king withdraws. There's no dissenting voice.
Each man comes forward to announce his choice:
Some with a flow of words that can't be stopped;
Some crisp, 'What he suggests I will adopt;'
Some weep, who knew Achilles as a boy;
Some who admired his prowess when at Troy.
The king returns. The priests declare the vote.
There is a ritual of words they chant by rote:
'Kings' reigns end with praise and loud ovation;
Kings' reigns begin with people's acclamation.
At dawn, the next new moon, Aphaia greets
The sun on her high cliff. Apollo meets
Achilles' waiting people for the shout
Of their approval. Let news be put about
That citizens should gather, see their king
Offer the prince his olive wreath, his ring,
The diadem. We'll make the sacrifice,
And at the temple, pledge the benefice.'

Achilles and the king count off the stars
That spin and dip around the pole; nothing mars
The sky or earth or calm reflecting sea.
They hardly talk. Peleus' thoughts range free;
Achilles thinks of what Apollo said,
And hears Apollo's music in his head.
'Look, the prick of dawn drives off the grey,

And brings Apollo's music with the day.'

The horses are nearby, always aware
Of when they're needed, saddled with the rare
Lustrous fleeces. Achilles mounts Xanthus,
Peleus on Pedasus; on Balius
Apomeros, as herald, rides ahead,
Conjuring stately poems in his head,
Fitting his words to the numinous strain
That fills the air, matching the high refrain
That meets them from those gathered at the shrine,
Sensing how nearly present the divine.
Achilles rides towards the eastern cliff,
Trembling and aching, apprehensive, stiff
In awful fear Apollo might not come,
Though in his head the pipes and lyres still hum.

Peleus stands high on the topmost stair,
Holds out the royal treasures, gleaming, rare.
The priests approach, singing the ovation,
The crowd shouts out full-throated acclamation.

Achilles and the sun arise together
To full view. Apollo's bright rays tether
The prince in light, clasped by the sun-god's arm,
Man without a shadow, immune from harm.
The people of Aegina see the nimbus
Contain their king as on Olympus.
Almost a god, almost the sun-god's equal,
Favoured by him to rule Aegina's people.
Imbuing him throughout with sacred kingship
As he accepts both diadem and friendship.

Apollo's beams fall in dazzling streaks
While to his ears alone the god's voice speaks.

'I watched while you at Delphi did not let
The aura of the place bemuse your spirit.'
The new king bows, and seems to meditate.
'You came back here, and now you hesitate?
Oh, Achilles, Troy will fall without you.
Troy must fall. It always was the great gods' vow.
Farewell. My light's too bright for mortal eyes.
You'll see me again, alarmed and in surprise.'

Achilles wakes from his trance, hears the crowd
Shout again, hail him, the king, himself, aloud:
'This is our hero, and Aphaia's friend.
May he reign in harmony time without end.'

'I will do what a king must do to keep
His state intact. Let disharmony not creep
Between you and your king. Keeping my word
Will be my pleasure. So, in our accord,
Let me pass my days without tears or grief
Or bitterness to spoil our shared belief.'

Apomeros

'Why, Achilles? You do not want me here?' 'Apomeros, I do.'

Later, Achilles calls for his poet,
  To sing and talk; and, with some small regret,
Outlines a project that he has in mind.
The young man's skills exceed what's here to find:
His voice in recitation soars aloud;
His audience, when he sings, becomes a crowd
Reduced to tears, or panting with the thrill
Of boars and panthers, heroes at the kill;
Gods coupling with girls, goddesses in love,
Mountainous giants clutching the skies above,

Despairing, desperate for remedy;
Mothers of sons beyond hope of recovery;
Priests at prayers, and gods working miracles;
Foul beasts winding sailors in tentacles
Stretched out from here to there and evermore,
While wives and children watch them from the shore;
Patience, endurance, courage, hate and lust;
Mountains and caverns, rapids, flash-floods, dust;
And ordinary tales of harvest feast,
Abundance and drought when rainfall ceased;
Cows and bulls and hairy-headed monsters;
Tricks and jokes pulled off by cruel pranksters;
And over all, the sky, the sea, the future,
All human life, seen as a huge adventure.

Apomeros, wondering what it's all about,
Thinks, perhaps what he's already written out
Honouring the kingship, acclamation
And the rest. He saw the visitation,
That godly light, and recognised its source;
The need for a grand epic he'll endorse.

But no. Achilles sits there. How will he give
His freedom to the poet? 'Sit by me.'
Apomeros wonders what it can be.
'Your poems are good, and our life here is good,
But is not worth a myth. I've understood
A long time that you need a bigger scene.
I grieve for Thetis too, our goddess queen,
Who cannot reconcile the life I chose
With what she dreamed for me. So I suppose
She wants her son at least to be a hero.
But I have become history's zero.
Apomeros, I will give you a task

At the far end of what a friend can ask:
Will you leave Aegina, and go to Troy,
And write a story time will not destroy?
Forget this little kingdom I now rule.
Use your imagination as a tool,
Tell a new story that will satisfy
Her need for heroism and its glory?
In the mist and dust of eternity
She may forget that I returned war-shy
To Aegina, had ceased to fight at Troy.
She needs the myth that glory will deploy
To hide the shame of my mortality,
Final disgrace of my fatality.'

They both sit silent. The young man's filled with fear.
'Why, Achilles? You do not want me here?'
'Apomeros, I do. But you have talent
For the wider world. Poetry is not meant
For trivia. There will be tales enough
To stretch all your belief into the rough
Wickedness of the worst of humankind,
And to the noblest sacrifice to find.
My heart comes near to breaking.'
                                                    'Mine too.
But, Lord Achilles, as is friendship's due,
I'll take up your commission. You took me,
Raw fish-boy, from the small Corinthian sea,
And brought me, following some whim or other,
Treated me as though I were your brother,
Gave me work, and a life-time's vocation.
Now I'll go, advocate of our nation,
To mould my language adept to your deeds,
For the flower of your epic, search out the seeds.

I'll gather the stories of the Trojan war,
Of kings and rivals, gratitude and gore,
And bundle them into a rolling epic
Of courage, steadfastness and panic.'
'Tell the tale with the old Achilles, not
The new. He makes a better story, hot
And rash, quarrelsome and vindictive.
Impossible that such a one should live.
You'll find that I was not an easy man.
And when at last the Fates cut my life's span,
Give me such death as satisfies my mother,
That, by the end of time, she may recover.'

Two men, no longer lord and servant, sleep
In their dreams: the younger, of the leap
Into the future he must take; the older,
Of how losing friendship makes life colder.
Two men share breakfast, barley bread and meat,
Honey and curded milk coaxed from the teat
Of palace goats.
                        The king picks up his theme.
'There is a man, part of the Aulis scheme,
Odysseus, who, curse him, understood me.
I hate and love and fear him, because he
Knew too much, and saw right in my heart
My flaws, had wisdom that he would impart
To do me good. But also much too clever
For me to bear, a bond I had to sever.
He's a bit flighty, he's a bit tricky,
Courts danger, situations dire and sticky,
A brand to fire the barley, brave and strong.
You'll not catch him sitting down for long.
But go make friends with him. Tell his horses

You rode Achilles' horse, pied Balius,
Knew Achilles. Then they will let you ride
To Odysseus' presence, boldly astride.
He is vain enough to want his story
Told by the finest. Do not be wary.
He will hear you out. Say (be brief, not long),
"A young poet is here, sings the gods' song,
Wishes to join your household, chronicling
Your deeds and journeys." I have an inkling
It will perhaps become a real commission:
Reckless living wildly excites his passion.'

Departure, change, mean quite different things
To the two men: for one, his life grows wings
To cross the sea, an end, but even more,
A new adventure on a distant shore.
But for the king, an end, another end
Of friendship, losing yet another friend.

Each man followed the path the gods defined:
Aegina's king ruled, always in his mind
The god's direction, allies make, not wars,
To right wrongs, give comfort, root out the cause,
And through a simple, quiet life make whole
Some of the damage poisoning his soul.
The other sang of wrath and devastation,
Proud poetry of hate and mad frustration;
Songs of the wily ways of politics;
Of sly Odysseus' devious antics;
Songs of chariots spinning round their foes,
And of the will of gods in the world's woes.
His tongue spoke of a catalogue of ships,
Described their crews and origins. His lips
Made poetry of numbers; set out fair

The true reporter's story: he was there.

At last, he went to Ithaca, overland,
And heard Odysseus' wild tale, told first-hand.

Achilles' End

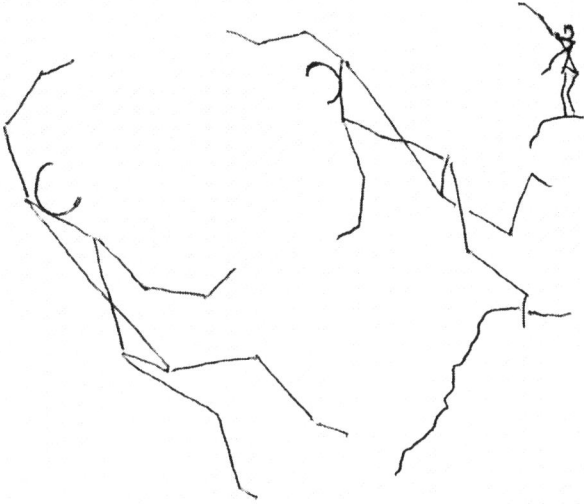

A vice of unforgiving stone... the mortal bone snaps

Years pass, many, the kingdom flourishes;
No wars, just occasional skirmishes
With mainland pirates, redundant fighters
From the eastern wars, mere overnighters
Before they're routed, sent back to Attica,
Or pacified, whichever means is quicker.
Aegina's commerce, produce and her stone
Acquire a reputation stands alone
In all the markets of the wide Greek world.
Merchants rush to the quays when they see furled

Her sails to slide her vessels into port,
To bargain for goods of the better sort.

Achilles married, raised heirs, such ordinary things,
While always entertaining princes and kings.
He never disclosed those nights of Stygian torment
When mutilated shades displayed their bellies rent
By his slashing sword cuts, their silent screams,
As their lifeless blood crimsoned Hades' lightless streams.
His household knew, knew when the man burdened by gloom
Shrank into himself as though unworthy of room
In the gay bustling world; Achilles, still waiting
For absolution from gods and men, debating
The benefits of death or immortality,
Reserve weighed against heroic brutality.
'For all Aegina's folks who saw me wear the crown
I have become Achilles, their king of no renown.'

For years Achilles ruled the land, uncounted years;
For years Thetis watched him, nursing unmeasured fears.
Her teeth, still pearly and perfect, sometimes flashed
Maternal pride in her fine son, but straightway dashed
With grim foreboding of the end of all old men:
Loss of their teeth, and loss of all their acumen.
He is perhaps a little restive, even bored.
His battle scars itch when news coming from abroad
Reaches his island; sometimes from Apomeros,
Perhaps of a death or triumph, sometimes the loss
Of cities, or in unknown seas of old companions.
And there have been worse: royal assassinations.
He knows now Troy was not his fight, was not his role.
The ends of those heroic lives cannot console
For the obscurity of his own achievement,
Or his mother's profound aching disappointment.

Apollo's oak trees drop their golden acorns;
Bristly boars flee hunted by resounding horns
As Thetis and Achilles, astride great horses,
Plunge through the thickets, each one in his courses,
Exhilarated and intent. At last they rest,
Blood pounding, joyous eyes, lips smiling, heaving chest,
Beneath a splendid oak. Acorns rain on their heads
Which Thetis gathers in her dress. 'Apollo sheds
His blessings. Let's follow him to the sunset edge,
Scatter out wide his fruits, and there renew the pledge.'

He stays her. 'There is unfinished business in my life.
Cuts me in two, a sharp-honed sacrificial knife.
My death, your disappointment must be reconciled,
Brought to terms lest our shared memory be defiled.
The life of every man ends in such a way,
Though desolate you're left to weep and pine each day.
Mother, there is a story. Find Apomeros.
He has his own means of diminishing your loss.
I do not think I merit immortality.
Between the gods and me there is no parity.'

His modesty rends his mother's heart. 'Come mount your horse.
Let's ride to that high cliff where I saw you arrive.'

And to herself, *Each moment while he's still alive*
Shall be an acorn to me, growing a memory
To last as long as can Apollo's mighty tree.

Out of the boar-dark wood, they ride the grassy sward
Of sheep-cropped turf as the sun slides rust-red downwards
To the mountains. At the cliff's edge, it's overgrown
Where rabbits scuttle in the rocks. Tangles and stone
Impede the horses' hooves. Achilles dismounts,
And ambles through the briars, musing as the sun flaunts

Direct into his eyes its horizontal ray.
This lingering sunset of Achilles' final day
Blinds him as forward step by step he ventures.
The briars become more tangled, root in the fissures
Between the rocks, until he can advance no more.
A trailing briar stops him, his foothold is unsure,
And at the fatal brink his ankle twists sideways,
Downwards, and there the grasping, quaking earth betrays
Its darker depth, a vice of unforgiving stone.
The cliff-edge crumbles,
Achilles stumbles,
And tumbles;
And in his dazzled ecstasy the mortal bone
Snaps. Momentum pitches him out and away,
Past crumbling rock and shattered scree to dying day
Through the light air; he's light as air; he's air and light,
Headlong into Apollo's outstretched arms. Tonight
There is no night,
Just the sight
Of the waiting god.
Apollo clasps Achilles; with his other arm
Salutes his mother. The god-man held in the calm
Of the god's embrace vanishes into his death.
He too raised an arm, waved at his final breath.
Sun and son are gone.
Her arm still raised, Thetis immobilised, pierced through
By the shards of a cutting comfort; all too true:
Death must come. She does not know which death were better:
The vengeful arrow splitting the ankle's fetter
To terminate an heroic life of violence,
Or the death of a man who loses his balance
In a common accident of normal life
After seventy years of pacifying strife.

What did they see, those hunters running from the wood
Alarmed by a single startled cry? Thetis stood,
Then stood no more. But in the sky-roads' dusky shrouds
Two figures, maybe three, three horses riding clouds.

Acknowledgements

I wish to thank my text editor, Wendy Turner, and my designer and typesetter, Ray Wilkinson, for their help, knowledge, advice and patience. I am grateful also to members of Verulam Writers (www.verulamwriters.org) for their advice in the decision on how to publish.